Smartphones

Martin Gitlin

Published in the United States of America by Cherry Lake Publishing
Ann Arbor, Michigan
www.cherrylakepublishing.com

Reading Adviser: Marla Conn, MS, Ed., Literacy specialist, Read-Ability, Inc.

Photo Credits: ©Artem Varnitsin/Shutterstock.com, cover, 1; ©Working in Paterson Project collection, 1993-2002 (AFC 1995/028), American Folklife Center, Library of Congress, 5; ©Rico Chen/Wikimedia/Creative Commons Attribution-Share Alike 3.0 Unported, 6; ©Paul Vlaar/Wikimedia/Creative Commons Attribution-Share Alike 3.0 Unported, 7; ©Mustaraamattu/Wikimedia/Creative Commons Attribution-Share Alike 3.0 Unported, 8; ©Michael Hicks/flickr, 11; ©Hakatanoshio117117/Wikimedia/Creative Commons Attribution-Share Alike 4.0 International, 12; ©Kansir/flickr, 13; ©Prostock-studio/Shutterstock.com, 14; ©Nemanja Zotovic/Shutterstock.com, 17; ©abalcazar/Shutterstock.com, 18; ©Soloviova Liudmyla/Shutterstock.com, 19; ©CJ Nattanai/Shutterstock.com, 23; ©EXTREME-PHOTOGRAPHER/iStock, 24; ©Aris Suwanmalee/Shutterstock.com, 25; ©Estrada Anton/Shutterstock.com, 27

Graphic Element Credits: ©Ohn Mar/Shutterstock.com, back cover, multiple interior pages; ©Dmitrieva Katerina/Shutterstock.com, back cover, multiple interior pages; ©advent/Shutterstock.com, back cover, front cover, multiple interior pages; ©Visual Generation/Shutterstock.com, multiple interior pages; ©anfisa focusova/Shutterstock.com, front cover, multiple interior pages; ©Babich Alexander/Shutterstock.com, back cover, front cover, multiple interior pages

Library of Congress Cataloging-in-Publication Data

Names: Gitlin, Martin, author.
Title: Smartphones / by Martin Gitlin.
Description: Ann Arbor : Cherry Lake Publishing, [2019] | Series: Disruptors in tech | Audience: Grades: 4 to 6. | Includes bibliographical references and index.
Identifiers: LCCN 2019006028 | ISBN 9781534147607 (hardcover) | ISBN 9781534150461 (pbk.) | ISBN 9781534149038 (pdf) | ISBN 9781534151895 (hosted ebook)
Subjects: LCSH: Smartphones—Social aspects—Juvenile literature. | Technological innovations—Juvenile literature.
Classification: LCC HE9713 .G528 2019 | DDC 384.5/3—dc23
LC record available at https://lccn.loc.gov/2019006028

Printed in the United States of America
Corporate Graphics

Martin Gitlin has written more than 150 educational books. He also won more than 45 awards during his 11-year career as a newspaper journalist. Gitlin lives in Cleveland, Ohio.

Table of Contents

CHAPTER ONE

How It Used to Be

An alarm clock woke up most people 50 years ago. Now a smartphone has taken its place.

A flashlight used to be the main tool for seeing in the dark. Now smartphones can provide that light.

In the past, people jotted down appointments on wall calendars. Now they use their smartphones to be reminded of events.

*Music lovers once placed records on turntables to hear their favorite songs. Now they **download** music to their smartphones.*

Taking pictures once meant carrying a camera and rolls of film. Today, smartphones can capture and store hundreds of images and video.

*Grabbing a ride in the city used to mean hailing a cab. Now opening an Uber or Lyft **app** on your smartphone will bring a ride right to you.*

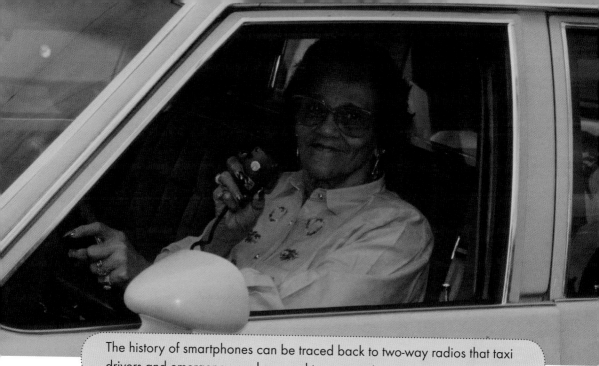

The history of smartphones can be traced back to two-way radios that taxi drivers and emergency workers used to communicate.

These examples only explain how smartphones have changed our routines for a few hours. But smartphones have altered most activities we do all day every day. They have changed how we work and play. They have changed how we communicate with friends and people we do not know. They have changed how we read and learn. They have changed how we shop. They have made lives easier.

In 1973, Motorola was the first company to mass produce cell phones for the public. It weighed a little over 2 pounds (1 kilogram)!

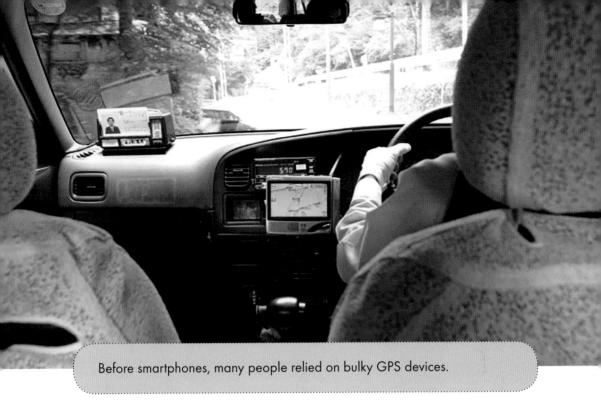

Before smartphones, many people relied on bulky GPS devices.

Smartphones Are Disruptive

Smartphones have also made **technologies** we once embraced **obsolete**. People no longer need radios because they can download apps of desired stations onto their phones. They've gotten rid of GPS devices because they can find destinations on Google Maps, an app on most smartphones. Some people have even dumped their desktops and laptops, and use their phones to surf the internet and send emails and texts.

It's no wonder that the smartphone has been called the most popular advancement in the history of technology. Its growth in less than a decade has been incredible.

The world's first SMS message, or text, was sent in 1992.

All About Bell

The smartphone could never have been created if not for the original phone. And the first phone would not have been possible without Alexander Graham Bell.

The telephone is considered one of the most important inventions of all time. Born in Scotland in 1847, Bell arrived in the United States to teach the deaf. He hatched the idea of electronic speech communication while visiting his hearing-impaired mother in Canada. He first invented the microphone. Then he developed what he called the "electrical speech machine." That became known as the telephone.

Bell received a **patent** for his invention on March 7, 1876. He transmitted actual speech 5 days later. He spoke into the phone to his assistant, Thomas Watson, who was in another room. Bell uttered his famous words: "Mr. Watson, come here. I need you." Those were the first words ever spoken into a telephone.

Bell died on August 2, 1922. On the day he was buried, all phone service in the United States was halted for one minute in his honor.

CHAPTER TWO

The Smartphone Boom

It was January 9, 2007. A week earlier, the world was ringing in the New Year. Now, Steve Jobs was giving folks something new to celebrate. The head of Apple Computer, Inc. unveiled the iPhone. He called it a breakthrough internet device.

The smartphone already existed. It came in the form of the BlackBerry. But BlackBerry users weren't able to do much other than send emails. The iPhone changed this. It introduced a newer and easier way of getting online. The internet was no longer limited to a computer at home or at the office. People could do online searches from anywhere.

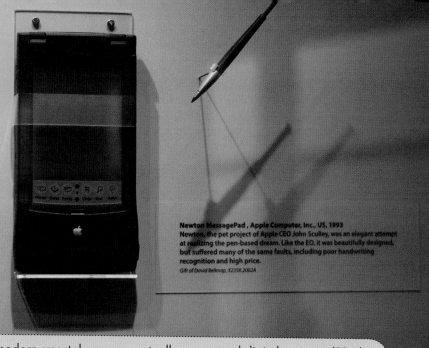

Newton MessagePad , Apple Computer, Inc., US, 1993
Newton, the pet project of Apple CEO John Sculley, was an elegant attempt at realizing the pen-based dream. Like the EO, it was beautifully designed, but suffered many of the same faults, including poor handwriting recognition and high price.
Gift of David Belknap, X2158.2002A

The first modern smartphone was actually a personal digital assistant (PDA). This was like a smartphone, without the phone feature.

Bye-Bye Phone Book

The iPhone changed everything. Its contact list feature allowed users to save favorite numbers and make calls simply by tapping on a name or number on the device's screen. And because you could also find business phone numbers through internet searchers, such as Google, you no longer needed a phone book!

Did you know that the iPhone introduced a "soft keyboard" that popped up only when you needed it? Before the iPhone, cell phones had a small keyboard. These weren't ideal for people with larger hands. The keyboards also added bulk to the phone and reduced the size of the phone's screen.

Many claim that the first camera phone was only available in Japan in 2000.

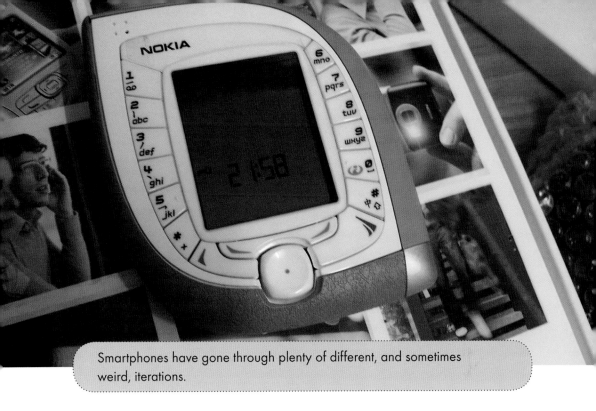

Smartphones have gone through plenty of different, and sometimes weird, iterations.

Voicemail Technology

The iPhone also featured a new option called Visual Voicemail. Instead of calling their voicemail and having to listen to all of the messages, people could use Visual Voicemail to view their messages all at once! Then they could listen to the ones they wanted to and immediately delete the others.

About 1 in 5 smartphone users primarily use their phones to go online.

Growing Number of Users

Some products take a while to catch on. But smartphones caught fire quickly. The number of American users increased by an incredible 45 percent from 2010 to 2011 alone—from 62 million to 93 million.

The rise in smartphone usage since then has been no less amazing. It soared by at least 18 million every year between 2011 and 2016. The number of users is estimated to reach nearly 271 million by 2022. That's nearly the entire population of the United States!

Some would say that smartphones have drastically changed the lives of all those users. And the world will never be the same because of it.

Great Jobs

Steve Jobs did not seem destined to grow into greatness. The man who co-founded Apple and built it into the world's most successful tech company was a college dropout.

Jobs was born in 1955. He grew up in California and showed a passion for electronics. He landed a summer job at Hewlett-Packard after requesting parts from that company for a school project.

His path took a detour a few years later. He dropped out of Reed College in Oregon after just one semester. He later quit one of his first jobs, designing video games for Atari. He instead decided to backpack through India.

The experience fueled his creative vision. Jobs returned to America. He teamed with friend Steve Wozniak to launch Apple Computer, Inc. Jobs sold his Volkswagen van to help finance the venture. The two built the Apple 1 computer in the garage of his parents' home. It had no keyboard or display. Customers were forced to assemble it themselves.

Jobs and his friends unveiled the Apple II computer a year later. It gained tremendous popularity. The rest is history. Jobs became one of the richest and most influential people in the world. Sadly, he lost his life to cancer in 2011.

CHAPTER THREE

The Good and the Bad

Smartphones have brought users closer to the outside world than ever before. The devices can be used by anyone anywhere to text or call. It just takes a few taps on the screen. People can find information about anything or entertain themselves while walking down the street or hanging out at home.

There's an App for That

The smartphone **revolution** has allowed businesses to better serve their customers. Their apps allow people to learn about what the businesses have to offer. Apps also provide news in the worlds of politics, entertainment, and sports with the touch of a finger. Users can get weather updates as they prepare to leave their homes or offices. No more guessing about whether or not to bring an umbrella.

While there is an app for almost anything, research indicates that 51 percent of smartphone users download zero apps a month!

In 2006, about 10 percent of households didn't have a landline and relied solely on their cellphone. In 2018, this number jumped to 53.9 percent.

What's Replaced?

The rise of smartphones has resulted in the fall of some technologies. Many have ditched their cameras and landline phones. Smartphones have replaced **portable** music players and game devices. The ability to download a variety of entertainment onto smartphones has made television and radio less popular.

New technologies often bring both good and bad results. The smartphone is no exception. We can only hope that the good outweighs the bad when history tells the whole story.

Using Bluetooth technology, smartphones can act as a video game controller for the Xbox or PlayStation. There are even video game controllers for smartphones.

The More We're Connected, the Less We Connect

But many believe smartphones have been a negative influence on **society**. One glance at any public place tells a disturbing story. Most folks are on their smartphones, scrolling through. They are not talking to each other. They are not reading newspapers or books. They are not going out as often with friends. They are not making as many new friends. Life has become more impersonal.

Smartphone use has impacted family life as well. Parents and kids often say nothing to each other. Their eyes and fingers are glued to their smartphones. No more dinner conversation. No more game nights at the dining room table. No more enjoying favorite TV shows together in front of actual televisions.

The negative effect of smartphones can be felt by millions. One can always work even when not in the office. That often leads to longer workweeks for the same pay. Newspapers have lost money and readers. Bookstores have gone out of business. The rise of driving services such as Uber and Lyft have hurt the taxi and bus industries.

Feeding Faces Through Smartphones

Among the most popular apps used by **millennials** are those that deliver food. Apps such as Grubhub, DoorDash, and Uber Eats have fed their need for speed and convenience.

A report released in June 2018 by investment bank UBS revealed that online food ordering services were exploding. The company predicted that delivery sales could rise to $365 billion by 2030. That forecast brought fear that people of the future would not do much cooking. After all, the report was titled "Is the Kitchen Dead?" Still, the number of restaurants that partnered with Uber Eats nearly tripled over a one-year period. Those that signed up included McDonald's and Buffalo Wild Wings.

What was most interesting about the report was that those born after 1980 were three times more likely to order from such services than their parents. It also showed that food delivery apps were among the top 40 most downloaded in major cities. The report predicted that more meals would be delivered than cooked in homes by 2030.

CHAPTER FOUR

A Worldwide Wonder

The 2018 Global Mobile Market Report revealed the incredible truth: Billions of people around the world use smartphones.

Leaders in Smartphones

Would you be surprised to know that the United States isn't the leader in smartphone ownership? In terms of numbers, China and India have the most people with smartphones. But they also have far more people living there than any other country in the world. In terms of country population, 94 percent of South Korean adults own a smartphone as of 2018. Compare this to the United States, where only about 77 percent of adults own a smartphone.

As of 2018, South Korea leads in smartphone usage. Almost 9 in 10 adults own one!

It's a Small World

Smartphones have shrunk the world. They have connected people from one side of the globe to the other. They have also shrunk our communities. Smartphones have changed the way we communicate and do business. Thousands of businesses have been created that allow people, with a simple tap on their phone, to buy products and have them delivered right to their door. Among them is Amazon, which has grown into an incredible force in the market.

Smartphones and apps have practically eliminated the need for webcams.

Smartphones have changed the way we shop.

Get Connected or Else

Businesses with little or no online presence are dying out. Malls and shopping centers are emptier than ever. Once-popular stores such as Sears, Kmart, JCPenney, and Toys"R"Us have either closed or are struggling to stay open. People are no longer stepping outside to make a purchase. In fact, some people are even buying cars on their smartphones!

Saving the Day

Thirty years ago, people away from their homes could only communicate through face-to-face contact or pay phones, if one was nearby. Smartphones allow people to connect with someone thousands of miles away—or learn about a news story as it breaks while they're walking down the street. They can also make an emergency call to a hospital for themselves or a loved one. These devices can indeed save lives.

Smartphones have changed the world and the people in it. How will smartphones be used in the future? When will they be used? How often will they be used? Will people start limiting their use and spend more quality time with family and friends? The answers to those questions will greatly impact the effect smartphones will have on the world.

The hugely popular *Fortnite*, a game of survival, was the most downloaded iPhone game in 2018. Placing second was *Helix Jump*, in which players navigate a falling ball through a maze. Ranking third was *Rise Up*, which allows players to protect a balloon from popping as it goes through obstacles.

What else will the smartphone replace?

Still Super Social

The rise of smartphones has not altered the favorite online activities of most Americans, according to a look at the most downloaded apps. The same social media sites embraced on personal computers remain popular on smartphones. That was the word from Apple in 2018. The company listed the most downloaded app that year as YouTube, a site that has been around since 2005. Other social media sites followed YouTube in number of downloads. But Facebook was no longer on top. It had fallen behind Instagram, Snapchat, and Messenger.

Timeline

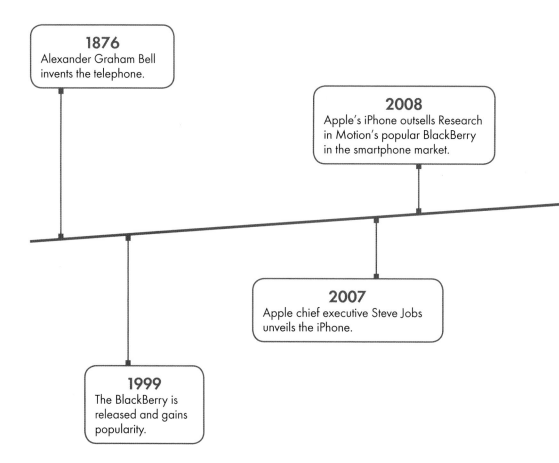

1876
Alexander Graham Bell invents the telephone.

2008
Apple's iPhone outsells Research in Motion's popular BlackBerry in the smartphone market.

2007
Apple chief executive Steve Jobs unveils the iPhone.

1999
The BlackBerry is released and gains popularity.

2010

February: Android phones compete with iPhones with the introduction of full touchscreen interaction.

June: Samsung Galaxy is released.

2016

Number of U.S. smartphone users soars over 200 million.

2011

Samsung becomes the best-selling smartphone, passing Apple in sales.

Learn More

Books

Greathead, Helen. *My Smartphone and Other Digital Accessories.* New York, NY: Crabtree Publishing, 2017.

Rogers, Sam. *Steve Jobs for Kids: A Biography of Steve Jobs Just for Kids!* Scotts Valley, CA: CreateSpace Independent Publishing Platform, 2013.

Websites

Inventive Kids

www.inventivekids.com

This site teaches kids about famous inventors and inventions and their own creative potential.

Science Kids

www.sciencekids.co.nz/sciencefacts/scientists/alexandergrahambell.html

This page provides cool facts about telephone inventor Alexander Graham Bell.

Glossary

app (AP) an application downloaded to a mobile device

download (DOUN-lohd) to transfer a capability to an app

millennials (muh-LEN-ee-uhlz) people born between 1981 to 1996

obsolete (ahb-suh-LEET) out-of-date; no longer used because something new has been invented

patent (PAT-uhnt) document giving an inventor sole rights to his or her invention

portable (POR-tuh-buhl) a device that is easily transported

revolution (rev-uh-LOO-shuhn) event that creates radical change

society (suh-SYE-ih-tee) an extended group that shares a cultural bond

technologies (tek-NAH-luh-jeez) modern inventions that have come from using science to solve problems

Index